Victims of Webcam Hacking 103: Ten Ways to Avoid Webcam Hacking

John Washington

ISBN: 0615927041
ISBN-13: 978-0615927046

www.CamiEyes.com

DEDICATION

Victims of Webcam Hackers

CONTENTS

ACKNOWLEDGMENTS

The Staff of CamiEyes, Inc.

www.CamiEyes.com

CHAPTER ONE
AVOID SUSPICIOUS WINDOWS

Have you been a victim of webcam hacking? This book discusses ten of the best ways to prevent becoming a victim. If you have been fortunate enough to be spared from the wrath of webcam hackers, these solutions will ensure that you will never fall into their trap. You will never see them coming; advisably follow these instructions and protect yourself from webcam hacking.

These 10 ways to prevent hackers from accessing your webcam in this book are meant to safeguard your privacy and ensure that even the most experienced of hackers have no chance in infiltrating your privacy. By following these ten ways of preventing webcam hacking, the webcam on your laptop or on your desktop will continue to be a useful device that will enable you to meet your obligations and spend quality time with your friends and relatives as opposed to it being a source of great personal pain.

As you browse through the internet, you probably have come across suspicious windows that are found on some websites. Clicking on these windows gives the hacker who planted the suspicious window access to your webcam. At all cost and no matter how enticing these windows are (most of them have captivating information that easily lures the computer owner into the hacker's trap), avoid clicking on them. The information visible to you in these windows is only meant to divert your attention;

the real and harmful information is contained underneath.

Click jacking is the technique applied in this scenario; by placing the “Allow” instruction directly beneath a captivating piece of information, more often a query, the hacker manages to entice the computer owner into clicking on this window and thus gains access to the computer’s webcam. Avoid clicking if you wish to stay out of the webcam hacker’s trap.

CHAPTER TWO
UPDATE YOUR OPERATING SYSTEM

The computer's operating system (OS) is viewed as the primary line of defense. In constantly updating the OS, you ensure that its definition especially on malware is ready to prevent computer hacking. Hackers are able to access a computer's webcam by using a somewhat superior coding to that of your operating system; your operating system is then instructed by the hackers to operate your webcam without your knowledge.

The operating system's update option is formulated to enable the computer user to keep tabs with the latest advances for the operating system. With each new update comes the ability to keep webcam hackers at bay. Frequently and periodically updating your computer or laptop's operating system will help to hold off these computer hackers.

CHAPTER THREE
SECURE YOUR WIRELESS NETWORK

Wireless networks can provide a hacker with a free pass to your computer and your webcam, which is the ultimate prize. If the hacker manages to maneuver their way into your wireless connection, they will have unlimited access to the resources therein and there is no telling how deep they will invade your private life. Securing your wireless connection will thus go a long way in ensuring that they do not gain access to your computer and webcam.

Ensure that your wireless network has a good password and an impregnable security settings to bar outsiders from tampering and subsequently accessing your network without your consent. Use lengthy and complex passwords when securing your wireless connection so you can block the computer hackers. Make sure you have a sound alert or a light that turns on near the webcam when it is operating.

Is your technical support trustworthy? The trustworthiness of the technician is the fourth way to avoid webcam hacking. Ask yourself this extremely crucial question. Hackers have real faces and identities and some of them do their hacking right in front of your face. Are you vigilant enough to identify these individuals posing as harmless computer technicians? Contact your wireless network provider before giving a technician access to your computer.

Some daring hackers pose as technicians and deceive the “client” into authorizing the use of hacking software on the computer. This software later turns out to be viral and it grants the hackers access to your webcam from where they can inflict immense damage as they intrude into your private life. Don’t just invite anyone posing as a computer technician; ensure that the technician is operating under a licensed company.

CHAPTER FOUR
USING CAMIEYES™ WEBCAM COVERS

The CamiEyes™ webcam cover is a fun way to cover the lens of the webcam. It eliminates the need for sophisticated and expensive firewall software that the computer hacker may find a way to get through anyway.

Some may say that webcam covers might be an out-of-dated way to block hackers, it serves its purpose pretty well. What is the easiest way to frustrate a webcam hacker than by literally blocking them completely? By placing a reusable cover on your webcam, you easily block off any uninvited viewers. These covers can be removed whenever the computer owner is using the webcam; they should be replaced as soon as the webcam is not being used. Although the CamiEyes™ serves its purpose well, it does not prevent the hacker from accessing the shared pictures taken using the webcam.

CHAPTER FIVE
CHECK YOUR WEBCAM LIGHT

The growing worry attributed to webcam hackers has forced laptop and external webcam companies into creating webcams that have indication lights that automatically light up whenever the webcam is active. By constantly and frequently checking whether the indication light is on, you will be able to identify whether someone is attempting to spy on you.

Most laptops are however equipped with faint indication lights which might go unnoticed; be vigilant and protect your private space aggressively by ensuring that the webcam indicator light is off whenever you are not using the device.

In addition to checking your indication light or using a webcam cover, you can close or fold your laptop or unplug your external webcam when you are not using it. Once you are done using your laptop, be it in the living room, bedroom or even at the office, close it; this is the safest way of ensuring that webcam hackers do not infiltrate your private space. Having closed your laptop, there is absolutely no perceivable way in which a hacker would gain access to your webcam and even if they did, what would be there for them to observe anyway?

This same precautionary measure applies to the owners of external webcams; once you are done using it, unplug it from the computer. The hacker will not have a direct connection to your webcam and as such, your privacy will be intact and safe from webcam hackers.

CHAPTER SIX
UPDATE YOUR FIRMWARE

There is an absolute need for each and every computer user to regularly update his or her software, it is advisable to do so since the most up to date software will always contain the recent security fixes that are essential for your laptop and computer's security.

Just like most of the stand-alone electronic devices in the office today, webcams are controlled by their firmware, and this is exactly where exposures are likely to be experienced. The relevance and formulations input in the development of firmware makes it vulnerable to manipulation by hackers.

Regular software updates are very important for the security of every computer program; they often contain new communication protocols to protect you against newly invented viruses and other privacy threats.

Webcam manufacturers are aware of loops and work towards alienating them; this is normally done by updating the existing firmware to fine-tune it and ensure that it is secure from manipulation by hackers. In order to avoid falling into the trap created by webcam hackers, it is advisable to constantly check for any updates on your firmware version and align your webcam with it. In so doing, hackers will have a hard time accessing your webcam and even when they do, you will have to update your firmware again;

it is a matter of who stays ahead in this grueling game.

CHAPTER SEVEN
KEEP FIREWALLS ON

Firewalls prevent unauthorized internet users from accessing private networks that are connected to the internet including your laptop or desktop computer. Firewalls can be implemented in both software and hardware; they basically block a third party from accessing your webcam.

Firewalls ensure that all unwanted and unwarranted traffic is blocked off and denied access to the computer and its components. Most of the unwarranted traffic includes hackers who want to gain access to your computer and webcam at whatever cost. Once inside your system, computer hackers will have the liberty and opportunity to access your private life and can even get hold of your sensitive personal information and documents.

Firewalls ensure that all the traffic getting inside the computer is legitimate and thus prevents most of the illegitimate entries. These entries, as expected, are made by computer hackers. Experienced hackers have however breached these firewalls. For most of the hackers however, they have a hard time breaching the firewalls and they eventually give up on bypassing the firewalls. Thus firewalls can go a long way safeguarding your privacy.

CHAPTER EIGHT
DISABLE WINDOWS REMOTE ACCESS

Have you disabled your remote access? Disable your Windows Remote Access immediately. If you disable the remote access, the hackers cannot access your computer using this remote route; they will have to be extremely good and use a very strong connection to alter it.

Here are the steps to disable the "Windows Remote Access" on your computer. First, click on the start button and locate "Computer". Then right click on the "Computer" and choose "Properties". On the left hand side, choose the "Remote Settings" option. Upon clicking on "Remote Settings", several tabs will appear. Choose the "Remote Option" and uncheck the dialog box that reads "Allow Remote Assistance Connections to this Computer". Finally under the "Remote" tab, choose the "Don't Allow Connections to this Computer" option.

CHAPTER NINE
WEBCAM PROTECTION SOFTWARE

There are several different software programs that can reside in the background of your laptop or computer. The programs notify you whenever your webcam is being used. The software control which programs are allowed to access your computer's webcam. Disallow online conversation programs or any other programs from using your webcam without your consent or approval. Set a unique password to bar everyone including your family members from using your webcam without your consent and permission.

By installing a webcam lock on your computer, you will be able to allow or block the access to the webcam for each and every program. Also you will be in a position that enables you to continuously know what program is attempting to access your webcam and you will be able to simply deny or allow that particular attempt. Installing a webcam lock goes a long way to protecting and safeguarding your privacy since each time a program tries to access the webcam, a confirmation window will pop up on the screen and at that instance you will be able to deny or allow the access.

Only the programs that you allow will be in a position to access the webcam. Once you have enabled access, an icon will be clearly displayed on the screen of your device reminding you that the recording is taking place. This is a great way to ensure that you are safe.

CHAPTER TEN
WEBCAM PROTECTION

If you have been a victim of webcam hacking, you will not continue jeopardizing your privacy by ignoring these recommendations. By implementing these ten ways of preventing webcam hacking, your privacy will no longer be subject to webcam hackers. The more precautionary measures you take towards ensuring that your computer is not hacked, the harder it will be for the hackers to gain access to your webcam. Each of these ten ways to prevent webcam hacking have been tried and tested; combining them makes it almost impossible for even the most experienced of hackers to gain control of your computer and webcam. Protecting yourself and your family aggressively from notorious webcam hackers will make you the victor and not the victim.

Create awareness and have your close acquaintances read this book to ensure that they are equipped with the necessary knowledge to enable them to deal with the menace that is bedeviling us today, webcam hacking.

WWW.CAMIEYES.COM

Made in the USA
Monee, IL
04 November 2026

67384418R10022

Victims of Webcam Hacking 102: Miss Teen America

John Washington

ISBN: 0615927068
ISBN-13: 978-0615927060

www.CamiEyes.com

DEDICATION

Teen Victims of Webcam Hackers

CONTENTS

ACKNOWLEDGMENTS

The Staff of CamiEyes, Inc.

www.CamiEyes.com

CHAPTER ONE
MISS TEEN AMERICA

Webcam hacking went mainstream after Miss Teen America became a victim of webcam hacking. Computer hackers are targeting celebrities and accessing their sensitive information on their computers. They then use this information to try to extort money from their victims in the form of blackmail. Protecting yourself from webcam hacking requires vigilance regardless of whether you are famous. You must avail yourself of all the precautionary strategies available to computer owners in order to block webcam hacking and protect your privacy.

As the public learned from this incident that befell this 19 year old celebrity, photographs can be taken using your webcam without the indicator light signalling it. Since some of the webcam applications have the option of switching off the indicator light as was the case with Miss Teen America's webcam, it then becomes necessary to employ other preventive measures such as placing a cover over your webcam. How exactly did Miss Teen America's laptop fall prey to hacking?

Gaining celebrity status is not what is use to be in light of the internet; Miss Teen America knows this now. Her troubles started when she became Teen California. A hacker managed to plant the Remote Administration Tool (RAT) application on her personal laptop. This tool gives the hacker control over the webcam and other sensitive files and documents. For a well-seasoned hacker, snapping pictures with the webcam indicator light off is an easy task; this is especially easy when the laptop or computer configurations allow for uninterrupted third party access.

In her own words during televised interviews, Miss Teen America confirmed that she was not aware of the hacker snapping and retrieving her pictures because the indicator light never alerted her. She has taken this webcam hacking incident as a challenge and is using her status to create awareness among teenagers in high schools and colleges. Were it not for an anonymous email she received demanding money from her, she would probably have never thought that she was being constantly monitored in her home.

Webcam hackers expose their victims to a myriad of mental and psychological torture as a way to extort their money. Miss Teen America, Cassidy Wolf, warns that all individuals with laptops and computers have to be mindful of their privacy by ensuring that hackers do not access their webcams and snap pictures that will be later used as blackmail. About four months prior to her webcam being hacked, Miss Cassidy Wolf had received a notification from a social media account stating that someone had tried to access her account from another state. This should serve as the first sign that webcam hackers are placing you under surveillance and laying their groundwork. Although the hacker did not hack the social media account, the hacker seemingly managed to plant the RAT on her laptop and thus gained access to her webcam and took pictures. The FBI took this issue very seriously and they quickly identified the hacker who committed this violation of privacy.

CHAPTER TWO
THE RAT

This disturbing application, the Remote Administration Tool (RAT), has evolved with time and it is now more accessible to hackers as a tool to spy on people. It is easy to use; as long as a hacker manages to install this virus on your computer, he or she has a relatively easy time accessing your privacy and placing you under surveillance even without your knowledge. As Miss Cassidy Wolf advocates, be aware of people who have access to your computer; their sole intention might be to install this disturbing application in order to extort money and subsequently ruin your reputation.

Uninstalling this virus is an hard task. Once it gets intertwined in your computer system, only an experienced and sharp technician would know how to get rid of it without compromising all your other files and documents. Hackers refer to their victims as "slaves"; this is after successfully installing the RAT application on their computers. So widespread has webcam hacking become that these hackers hold meetings and discuss their "slaves" as well as share tips. Miss Teen America is not taking this lightly; her spirited campaign is geared at empowering teenagers with information on how to avoid falling into the hacker's trap. The FBI has not slowed down in their investigation; they have made notable steps that will lead to the prosecution of the hacker responsible for planting the RAT application on her Miss Teen America's laptop.

As nature would have it, young women occupy the largest portion on the hackers' playbook and for a pretty obvious reason. Using the RAT, a hacker takes nude pictures of the female victim and then demands money or other forms of compensation. It is Miss Cassidy Wolf's hope that teens will learn from her horrific experience and avoid falling into the hacker's trap altogether. Having your nude pictures flagged all over the internet is very disturbing; the affected individual may have to undergo a series of therapeutic sessions in order to overcome the embarrassment that comes with this kind of unwarranted publicity. As a celebrity, Cassidy Wolf is even more vulnerable to extortion; had the hacker not been arrested, her career would no doubt have suffered greatly.

CHAPTER THREE
SAFEGUARD YOURSELF WITH CAMIEYES™

Miss Cassidy Wolf advises teens to protect their privacy at all costs. When you have had a gruelling day be it at work or at school, what is that one place that gives you uninterrupted peace and comfort? It is usually your bedroom, your private space. If a hacker manages to install RAT on your laptop, you will unknowingly lose this kind of privacy. There are various ways of ensuring that your private space remains as such. There are a few tips on how to steer clear of computer hackers.

First, put a CamiEyes™ webcam cover over the lens of your webcam. CamiEyes is a fun webcam cover for the entire family.

Miss Wolf has been categorical in stating that she has resorted to covering her webcam whenever she is not using it. This might seem like an extreme move but when it comes to one's own privacy, it is a small price to pay. By covering your webcam, the hacker on the other end won't be able to view your activities even if the RAT application is functioning.

Second, don't be click happy. As you browse through websites, do you occasionally come across constantly moving windows that are often in the form of a query? You should try to avoid clicking on these websites because it may grant the hacker access to your computer. These suspicious windows employ a click jacking technique; by placing the "Allow" command directly beneath it, the victim clicks on it without knowing that he or she is granting the hacker access to his or her webcam and other files contained on his or her computer.

Third, be aware of the credentials of the technicians help you with your computer network. Hackers are known to form affiliate groups with computer technicians; alternatively, they themselves can pose as technicians. If they manage to get hold of your computer, they may plant the RAT application on your computer and thereafter use it to try to extort money from you. It is always advisable to hire the services of a registered company; in case there is an inconsistency in your system, they will be held accountable. These and other methods of preventing webcam hacking are being championed by the passionate Miss Teen America; her campaign will ultimately yield the desired results in the long run.

CHAPTER FOUR
THE FBI

After the Federal Bureau of Investigations (FBI) conclusively carried out their investigation, they singled out a 19 year old hacker as the source of miss Wolf's woes. Jared James Abrahams, a computer science student in California, joined hack forums as a way of gaining fame among his fellow hackers. Before Miss Wolf rose to fame, the two apparently attended the same school.

The young hacker planted the RAT application on Miss Teen America's laptop in 2012. He was able to get access to her webcam and take nude pictures of her in the privacy of her home. He then tried to access her social media accounts; this led to the various accounts notifying her of the violations coming from out of state. Since Miss Wolf had already claimed the Teen California title earlier in her career, she became a high-value target for hackers like Jared James Abrahams.

The 19 year old hacker admitted in the hacking forums that he wasn't excelling in social engineering. So he wanted to prove his hacking skills to his fellow hackers. In the present day world, you will be surprised to know that hacking has gone hi-tech and is a profitable business. Were it not profitable, why would hackers risk arrest? The law finally caught up with this young man who unfortunately bought into the culture of the hacking forums . The judge hearing his case stated categorically that hacking is illegal and as a way of reinforcing that, Jared was slapped with a $50,000 bond; a hefty amount indeed.

Having been an avid and active participant in hacking forums, Jared had quite a number of resources and technical help at his exposure. In these forums, hackers try to outdo each other and determine who reigns supreme in the hacking world. It appears that Jared was determined to shine and be recognized among the top hackers.

When hackers introduced the RAT application into the hacking forums, it became relatively easy for hackers to gain control of their victims' webcams. Jared's venture into this new territory with RAT gave him access to Miss Wolf's computer.

After thorough investigations, the FBI realized that this young man had a total of 150 victims worldwide.

This is a relatively high number of victims. If they all decided to file charges against Jared, he will have at least 150 charges to contend with as a result of his hacking. By the time he planted the RAT application on Miss Wolf's computer, she was a teen model working her way to the top. When she arrived at the top, Jared was in a very good position to gain fame and accolades from his fellow hackers. Jared's family has officially apologized to Miss Wolf and all the other victims of Jared's hacking and blackmailing. Miss Teen America has certainly not suffered in her career; on the contrary, her elevated position enables her to create awareness on a national level to make teenagers aware of the proliferation of webcam hacking worldwide. Jared on the other hand represents the face of troubled individuals who make it their objective to intrude into people's privacy and even demand monetary compensation or face the publicizing of the nude pictures or other personal documents accessed by the hacker.

CHAPTER FIVE
THE HACKER

On May 17, 2012, Jared James Abrahams, a 19 year old hacker , announced his computer hacking success to the RAT Community stating that although he sucked at social engineering, he had been lucky enough to infect a fellow student's laptop with RAT. As the authorities would later learn in their yearlong investigation, the student in question is Miss Cassidy Wolf, a teen model at the time. As she gained popularity, so did Jared in the hacking forums.

Wolf's privacy had been grossly violated since then; she was not even mildly aware of the violations. Jared had managed to access her webcam and snapped nude pictures of her even without the indicator light on her webcam turning on during the recordings.

The RAT application enables the user to turn off the webcam light and take pictures without the victim's knowledge. The intrusion of privacy is a crime. The FBI managed to single out 150 other victims, some of whom are from other countries; that is how widespread computer hacking has become. The internet is a powerful tool that can be used for good but has been used for bad in the life of this young woman. Taking nude pictures using the webcam unbeknownst to the victim is a task which requires computer expertise. Jared may not be good at social engineering as stated by him, but his hacking skills allowed him to continually monitor at least 150 victims. Due to Miss Wolf's fame, influence and public stature, she became Jared's primary target.

CHAPTER SIX
THE BLACKMAIL

Do not comply with the demands of extortion by webcam hackers. Notify the authorities immediately. In her new position the Miss Teen America, Cassidy Wolf made the right choice and notified the FBI of her violation and extortion This is definitely setting the right example for other teenagers who look up to her. Individuals are thus advised to follow this same path to ensure that the hackers responsible for trying to extort money from them are arrested and prosecuted to the fullest extent of the law. The hope is that the outcome of reporting these hackers to authorities will cause more and more hackers to abandon their trade and turn to legal computer work.

Jared had successfully accessed one of Wolf's social media accounts and posted a half nude photo of her. As Wolf was trying to digest all this, she received an anonymous email from Jared who had a couple of demands. He required Miss Wolf to send him more nude photos of her and to make a five minute appearance with him online. Had she complied with his demands, the results would have been devastating as Jared would have gone to any lengths to keep her in his grip. If he had a whole new set of nude photos, Jared would have the ultimate control over Miss Teen America. He would have continued with the extortion. Giving into hackers' demands is the greatest mistake one could make and Miss Wolf's character was strong enough; she made the right decision and as a result of that, Jared is in custody and awaiting a trial.

The presiding Judge will without a doubt want to make an example of Jared since this has become a national and global problem; webcam hacking has to be neutralize before it advances any further. With the arrest of Jared, his fellow hackers also risk exposure. The FBI and other security organizations will definitely work towards dismantling the hacking forums; a hard task which will have to be done by legitimate and superior hackers. The recent success attributed to Miss Cassidy Wolf is a huge step towards fostering privacy. Having your nude pictures splashed all over the internet can pretty much ruin a good reputation and leave the victim utterly devastated.

CHAPTER SEVEN
UNMASKING THE HACKER

On March 29th 2013, FBI found out that Miss Wolf's laptop had been infected with RAT. This discovery explained how Jared was able to take webcam pictures without being detected by Miss Wolf. The emails that had been sent to Miss Teen America demanding more nude photos could not be traced back to the sender since the VPN used kept no logs. This did little to deter the FBI's investigative spirit; by accessing a VPN online service, RAT had contacted Jared. By following up with this online service, the FBI was able to find the identity of the hacker who had repeatedly threatened Miss Teen America. Jared had opened an account using his father's legal name. As the FBI deepened their investigations, they realized that Miss Wolf wasn't Jared's only victim. Some of his victims live in Canada and Ireland. Some had already complied with his demands and stripped naked online.

An Irish woman had pleaded with Jared to stop blackmailing her but her pleads fell on his deaf ears. Thanks to the efforts made by the self-driven Miss Teen America, the Irish woman and other victims will get justice. Intruding into people's privacy and then extorting money from them all in the name of hacking has to stop. It is a saddening trend that appears to be growing.

Miss Teen America has stated that she will see this through to the end. By creating awareness of hackers like Jared, teens and adults alike will know how to protect their privacy and avoid falling into the traps set by these cunning hackers. On May 27th, Jared once again contacted Miss Wolf and threatened to splash her nude photographs all over the internet and through a number of social media accounts he had already gained control. Because of the swift efforts made by the FBI, her dignity and privacy remains intact. This was however not the case for some of Jared's victims; those who had already given into his demands. Had Miss Wolf remained silent on this matter, her hard earned reputation and status would have gone down the drain. In order to deal with hackers effectively and conclusively, it is best to confront them through security organizations such as the FBI.

As Jared faces possible jail time and fines, Miss Teen America is making appearances on talk shows and empowering teens who have already fallen prey to webcam hackers. Her efforts are expected to build a lot of positive energy among her fans; people are increasingly becoming aware of the dangers their laptops and computers can cause them.

Your privacy can only be protected by you. Ensure that whenever you are not using your laptop or computer, the webcam is either covered with a webcam cover like CamiEyes™ or unplug it. Your life should not be interrupted by computer hackers like Jared James Abrahams. In closing, enjoy your social life to the fullest on the internet but make sure that you take all the necessary precautions to minimize the possibility of your privacy being compromised without your knowledge. Cover it up!

WWW.CAMIEYES.COM

Made in the USA
Monee, IL
04 November 2026

67384422R10022